LEAGUE
OF
LEGENDS

KENNY ABDO

Fly!
An Imprint of Abdo Zoom
abdobooks.com

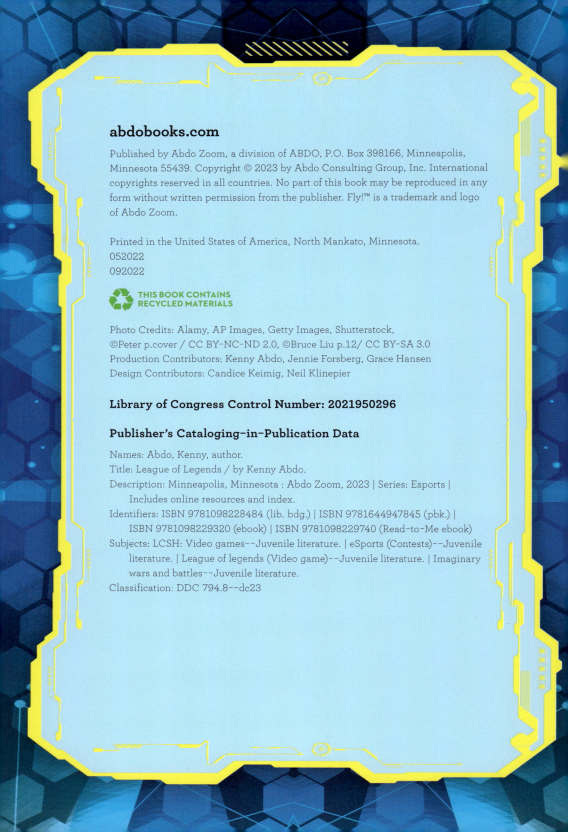

abdobooks.com

Published by Abdo Zoom, a division of ABDO, P.O. Box 398166, Minneapolis, Minnesota 55439. Copyright © 2023 by Abdo Consulting Group, Inc. International copyrights reserved in all countries. No part of this book may be reproduced in any form without written permission from the publisher. Fly!™ is a trademark and logo of Abdo Zoom.

Printed in the United States of America, North Mankato, Minnesota.
052022
092022

Photo Credits: Alamy, AP Images, Getty Images, Shutterstock, ©Peter p.cover / CC BY-NC-ND 2.0, ©Bruce Liu p.12/ CC BY-SA 3.0
Production Contributors: Kenny Abdo, Jennie Forsberg, Grace Hansen
Design Contributors: Candice Keimig, Neil Klinepier

Library of Congress Control Number: 2021950296

Publisher's Cataloging-in-Publication Data

Names: Abdo, Kenny, author.
Title: League of Legends / by Kenny Abdo.
Description: Minneapolis, Minnesota : Abdo Zoom, 2023 | Series: Esports | Includes online resources and index.
Identifiers: ISBN 9781098228484 (lib. bdg.) | ISBN 9781644947845 (pbk.) | ISBN 9781098229320 (ebook) | ISBN 9781098229740 (Read-to-Me ebook)
Subjects: LCSH: Video games--Juvenile literature. | eSports (Contests)--Juvenile literature. | League of legends (Video game)--Juvenile literature. | Imaginary wars and battles--Juvenile literature.
Classification: DDC 794.8--dc23

TABLE OF CONTENTS

LEAGUE OF LEGENDS

With endless new events, **tournaments**, and **champions**, *League of Legends* (*LoL*) has become one of the most played games in the world.

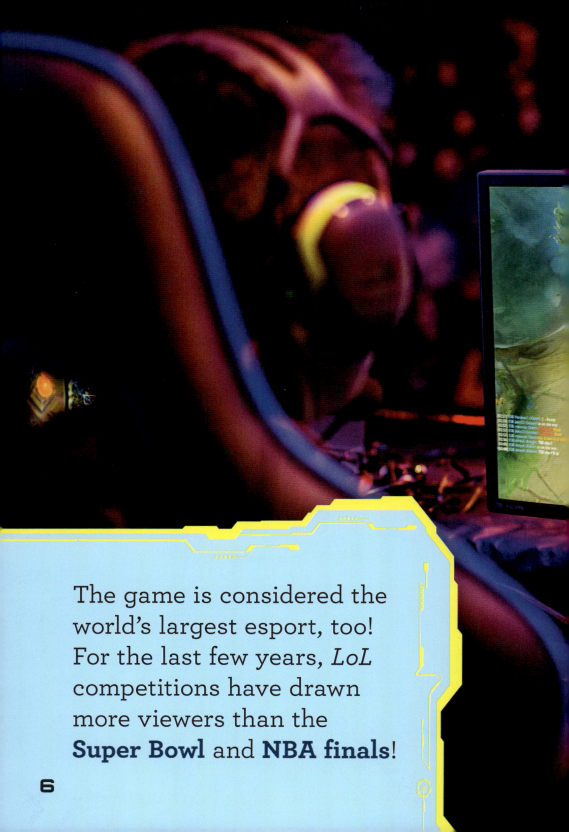

The game is considered the world's largest esport, too! For the last few years, *LoL* competitions have drawn more viewers than the **Super Bowl** and **NBA finals**!

Riot Games founders Marc Merrill and Brandon Beck wanted to make something new. The team set its sights on creating a standalone, free-to-play, multiplayer game.

League of Legends was released in 2009. It was an instant success! Players liked being able to customize their **champions**, and the game's open maps and regular **patches**.

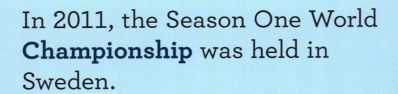

In 2011, the Season One World **Championship** was held in Sweden.

Watched by 1.6 million people, team Fnatic beat squads from all over the world!

JOURNEY

In 2013, Riot created the League of Legends **Championship** Series (LCS). It is a yearly competition where 10 teams fight for the chance to play at the LoL World Championship.

Lee "Faker" Sang-hyeok is considered the best *LoL* esports athlete in the history of the game. He began his career in 2013 and became the World Champion that year. Faker won again in 2015 and 2016.

FunPlus Phoenix was the 2019 World **Championship** victor. More than 100 million people watched online. That was more views than the **Super Bowl**!

Team DAMWON Gaming was the World Champion in 2020. Beating 21 other teams, DAMWON's **jungler** Kim 'Canyon' Geon-bu was crowned **MVP**!

As of 2021, *LoL* has 115 million active monthly users. It also has around 50 million daily active players. That is more than the population of some countries!

Riot's head of esports Chris Hopper sees a bright future for the game. He is working on making *LoL* an official high school varsity sport and having college competitions that offer scholarships.

The number of *LoL* players grow each year. It has steadily risen ever since the game was first released, proving that the legend will always live on.

GLOSSARY

champion – player controlled characters. Each champion has unique skills, abilities, and traits.

championship – a game held to find a first-place winner.

jungler – a type of champion that stays mostly in the jungle. They help their team with targets whenever possible.

MVP – short for Most Valuable Player, an award that is given to the best performing esport athlete.

NBA Finals – the championship series of the NBA where the team who wins best-of-seven games is determined champions of the year.

patch – a change made to update, fix, and improve a game.

Super Bowl – the NFL championship game, played once a year.

tournament – a set of games or matches held to find a first-place winner.

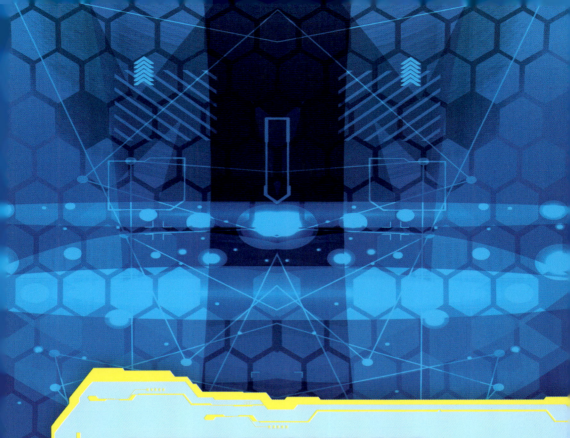

ONLINE RESOURCES

Booklinks
NONFICTION NETWORK
FREE! ONLINE NONFICTION RESOURCES

To learn more about League of Legends, please visit **abdobooklinks.com** or scan this QR code. These links are routinely monitored and updated to provide the most current information available.

INDEX